NIST Special Publication 500-280

Mobile ID Device
Best Practice Recommendation
Version 1.0

Shahram Orandi
R. Michael McCabe

Information Access Division
Information Technology Laboratory

July 2009

National Institute of Standards and Technology
Technology Administration, U.S. Department of Commerce

Mobile ID Device Best Practice Recommendation Version 1.0

Shahram Orandi
U.S. Department of Commerce
Technology Administration
National Institute of Standards and Technology
Information Technology Lab
Gaithersburg, MD 20899

R. Michael McCabe
ID Technology Partners, Inc.
Gaithersburg, MD 20877

July 2009

U.S. Department of Commerce
Gary Locke, Secretary

National Institute of Standards and Technology
Patrick D. Gallagher, Deputy Director

Acknowledgements

We would like to acknowledge and thank Scott Swann of the Federal Bureau of Investigation's (FBI) Criminal Justice Information Services (CJIS) Division as well as other key partners at the FBI who provided support to both NIST and Identification Technology Partners (IDTP) on the development of this Mobile ID Best Practice Recommendation.

Additionally, we would like to acknowledge the significant contributions made to the development of this document by Dale Hapeman BTF/BAH), Peter Higgins, Udo Mahlmeister (L1), Rick Lazarick (CSC), Anthony Mislin (L1), and Ambika Suman (NPIA/UK).   These individuals provided the text for various portions of the document.

Finally, we would also like to give special thanks to those who participated in one or more of the workshops that were held and to those who provided valuable editorial comments and suggestions used in shaping and completing this document.

This effort was supported with funding provided by the FBI and NIST.

Table of Contents

Figures

Tables

1 Introduction

The term "Mobile ID" can conjure up several different interpretations. In the strictest sense, it may consist of an un-tethered device used to capture one or more biometric samples from a subject. The captured data sample(s) may then be compared to other samples contained in a database resident on that device. The data may also be transmitted to and compared to samples in a central repository or an onboard computer repository located in a nearby vehicle. Such vehicles may include jurisdictional police cars, border patrol vehicles, military combat vehicles such as Humvees[1], etc. This scenario allows for comparison to larger databases than otherwise available on a handheld device or in a nearby vehicle. Additionally, a device physically attached to a computer located in a vehicle that acquires biometric samples may also be considered as a Mobile ID device.

For purposes of this report, the exact definition or categorization of the Mobile ID device is not a factor. The Mobile ID device should be viewed in the context of a portable biometric acquisition station – one that is not intended to be stationary and hardwired to a much larger system used for comparing or matching biometric samples. This is in contrast to traditional booking stations and other biometric enrollment stations incorporating physically secured full-sized live-scan fingerprint readers, other biometric modality capture devices, or photo capture stations with setups adhering to distance, lighting, and other photo capture standards.

Over the past several years Mobile ID devices and systems have been employed for various applications. In the FBI and law enforcement environment these devices enable an officer to acquire a subject's fingerprints, facial image or other biometric at a variety of different physical locations. In the DoD world they are used for identity verification of foreign workers, access control to secured communities and bases, and for ad-hoc checkpoint operations. For both of these environments, once the biometric sample is acquired, comparisons can be made with other biometric samples on watch lists and databases. This can all be done in near real time on the streets or at a remote location without the need of transporting the subject to a central office - with much less inconvenience to those involved. The result is a zero transit time other than for subjects identified as persons of interest to be retained for further processing. In the DHS environment, aspects of the US VISIT program to screen foreign visitors, the TWIC program for verifying transportation workers, and across all Departments, the PIV program for uniform civilian credentialing may be relying more on

---

[1] Specific hardware and or software products identified in this report were used in order to describe specific use cases and/or scenarios. In no case does such identification imply recommendation or endorsement by the National Institute of Standards and Technology, nor does it imply that the products and equipment identified are necessarily the best available for the purpose.

Mobile ID devices in the future. In the DHS environment, the subject is motivated to be verified in order to obtain access to the US, a service, facility, or computer. If a match is not found, one or more access rights or privileges may be denied depending on the application or database searched. Another application of Mobile ID devices is related to the new electronic identity documents that contain, in a contact or contact-less chip, one or more biometric samples (fingerprint, facial image). By using a Mobile ID device, a fast identity verification can be performed by comparing the live fingerprint of the person in possession of the document with the owner's fingerprint stored in the document chip, and, if needed, the captured biometric sample can be sent to a central system for further checks. Like the DHS environments this electronic identity documents application differs from law enforcement or DoD due to the motivational nature of the subject.

Currently, manufacturers are producing devices used to acquire fingerprint, face, and iris images but additional biometrics, such as voice, are currently being added to specific applications (i.e., DoD systems) or being planned for the future. Unfortunately, data acquired from a device using one system cannot always be read or processed by another system. In the case of fingerprints, this may be the result of different scanning resolutions, retention of image versus template, use of different image sizes, or use of different fingers. Such a variety of characteristics can result in a general lack of interoperability between systems.

Agencies want to search other systems without regard to existing dissimilarities between vendor systems. The FBI is piloting a new rapid search system based on the Repository for Individuals of Special Concern (RISC) that provides access to current national wants, warrants, known or suspected terrorists, and other individuals of interest. Additionally, the defense community wants the war-fighter to be able to search DoD, FBI, and DHS repositories. In order to satisfy these goals, common interoperability requirements must exist at the local, state, and federal levels. Although such requirements are in place at the central facility level, such as an ABIS, they have not yet been developed or applied at the mobile biometric capture device level.

To accommodate these needs, the Advisory Policy Board (APB) to the FBI's CJIS division approved a request to develop a set of guidance principles for biometric system applications of mobile identification systems. This has served as the impetus to develop a suite of Mobile ID Device Best Practice Recommendations (BPR) keyed to generic use cases for the law enforcement, defense, and homeland security applications. These recommendations focus on the capture and exchange of fingerprint, face, and iris images rather than templates consisting of characteristics derived from vendor-processed images. Although this BPR provides an option for fingerprint minutiae templates for identification applications, the use of captured images produces more accurate results when data is exchanged between dissimilar systems. Since there are, however, already a number of installed systems that are providing good value and cannot summarily be ruled obsolete, and since the technology is continually redefining what is possible, a roadmap forward can be designed and developed to progressively "raise the bar" to improve interoperability, biometric quality, and accuracy while providing for backward compatibility with existing systems. As the Mobile ID devices improve and current systems need to be replaced, replacement systems can be procured to adhere to higher performance standards. Such an approach will accommodate the largest possible group of current systems and will provide good future options as technology evolves.

Rather than creating a single standard to accomplish this, the strategy will be to develop a series of profiles or sets of best practices for each biometric modality. These profiles are intended to list device characteristics, software, security, and communication settings recommended for specific levels of performance. Defining these profiles will make it possible to accommodate most existing systems while providing richer opportunities for the next upgrade.

This document does not directly specify the capabilities or performance of the local or central database or repository. Those requirements are driven by the particular problem being solved.

2 Scope

This document is primarily targeted at law enforcement, criminal justice, military, homeland security, and other applications demanding a high degree of accuracy in the enrollment, identification, and verification functions. The focus of this BPR is not only on the Mobile ID device itself, but also on its connection to broader secure systems. Often, these applications have subjects that are not willing or able to provide trusted identity information. Whether cooperative or uncooperative, the resulting biometric identification needs to provide a reasonable degree of certainty that it will stand up to scrutiny including potential audits of security access control systems or the possible court challenges. This BPR is not designed or intended for consumer devices or other commercial applications requiring only minimal levels of accuracy and reliability.

Biometric capture devices addressed by this BPR will be limited to those capable of acquiring one or more modalities of fingerprint, facial, or iris image data. A series of Biometric Acquisition Profiles (BAP) are used to describe sets of best practice recommendations for specific biometric modalities intended to improve the capture, interoperability, and quality of the biometric data obtained from Mobile ID capture devices.

Within each particular modality, a series of Subject Acquisition Profiles (SAP) will identify progressively more stringent sets of parameters and requirements relevant to that device and modality. The concept of the SAP has its foundation in the Type-10 record of the ANSI/NIST standard. It is a convenient way to group and denote a series parameters associated with a particular capture device. These profiles are identified by numerical levels in this document. Lower SAP numbers indicate currently available and operational systems.

Higher values indicate stricter requirements available in "higher-end" or future systems. As the SAP numbers increase, so do the capabilities of the device.

The SAP levels used are examined in light of their intended functional use for enrollment, identification, or verification purposes. The enrollment process should always require a more stringent set of requirements. Verification may not require the same stringent set of parameters used for identification or enrollment.[2] In addition to considering the intended function, when setting an SAP level for a particular BAP, the potential risk factor to public safety must also be determined. The evaluation of a severe, moderate, or mild risk factor for each function must be made based on operational needs.

3 Purpose

This BPR provides guidelines for the capture (Sections 6-8), use (Section 9), security (Section 11), and transmission (Section 12) of mobile identification data that can be interoperable with similar and dissimilar systems. It also provides guidelines for environmental requirements for Mobile ID devices (Section 13). This BPR has been developed for government applications and is intended to be used with both open and proprietary systems with the goal of promoting interoperability and data exchange. Use of the SAP levels provides the analyst with a tool for tailoring the capabilities of a Mobile ID device to the individual enrollment, identification, or verification functions required. A Mobile ID device application may call for the same SAP level for all functions. Or it may require a more stringent level for the enrollment with a relaxed SAP level for verification. Choice of the levels will depend on the overall system application. Any collection device rated at the same or higher SAP level would be appropriate for a given biometric system application functional profile.

This BPR defines parameters addressing the content, format, and units of measurement for the exchange of biometric sample information for each combination of biometric capture device, function, and SAP level. Information consists of a variety of mandatory and optional information items such as fingerprint scanning resolution, pixel distances between facial features, and compression algorithm information for each biometric modality.

This document is intended to assist those organizations that process and exchange fingerprint, facial, and iris biometric data captured and acquired from a Mobile ID device without regard to any peculiarities of that device. Information captured, compiled and formatted in accordance with this BPR and compliant with the target system's

---

[2] Tactical uses by the DoD and others might be in operationally challenging situations where full capture of all biometric samples defined in a BAP level are not always possible – this does not go against the spirit of the recommended BAP

implementation of the ANSI/NIST-ITL 1-2007 or ANSI/NIST-ITL 2-2008 can be transmitted and seamlessly exchanged.

For those systems requiring connectivity with systems based on the FBI's IAFIS or NGI, these profiles will rely on the FBI's current version of the EBTS [formerly EFTS] in addition to the ANSI/NIST-ITL standard; the EBTS specifies record types with field requirements that are based on existing and planned systems. For connectivity with non-FBI based systems, the profiles must be compliant with the target system's EBTS or other application profile interface.

4 Applicability

Mobile ID devices have been employed for a variety of applications where a stationary booking station type environment is not possible or easily attainable. Common applications include:

- The officer on the street or the soldier at a checkpoint who needs to perform a quick check against one or more biometric databases and/or watch-lists
- Security at high profile, major public events, where fixed ID systems may not be practical or appropriate
- Issuance of a citation that requires registration of the biometric with the incident
- Enforcement of arrest warrants
- Verification of the identity of subjects at court appearances
- Access control for buildings, computers and networks, both for subjects seeking access as well as to authenticate the operator of the mobile device itself
- Security involving prisoner transport and release tracking
- Immigration and border control
- Entitlement programs and job applications

This technology is also being used by the DoD to monitor activities and/or determine any interaction with known or suspected terrorists (known as KSTs).

These applications and others are being accomplished with on-the-spot acquisitions of fingerprints and/or "mug shots" for comparison with samples stored in key databases. Although iris comparison has not been identified as a current application for law enforcement applications, this technology is under consideration at some agencies and mobile enrollment of irises is already standard practice in many military scenarios. The SAP levels required for each device must be tailored to the application it is being used for and also evaluated in terms of enrollment, identification, and verification requirements. The more critical the application is in terms of acceptable performance errors, the more restrictive the BAP needs to be.

5 Architectural Considerations

5.1 Tasks

There are several tasks to be accomplished by a biometric mobile identification system. The primary ones include image capture, signal or image processing, matching, and ultimately, an output decision that indicates an action to be taken by the operator. This action is based on an application specific decision process. Figure 1 illustrates typical combinations of these tasks across four basic scenarios that can be used to divide the workload up between the Mobile ID device and a networked system.

The objectives to be accomplished for each of the tasks are:
- Data Capture – The process of acquiring one or more raw biometric samples from a subject
- Signal Processing - Process of extracting distinguishing features from a raw biometric sample - this may include some or all of the following:
  - image normalization
  - segmentation
  - feature extraction
  - quality assessment
  - template creation

- Matching - The process of comparing the features extracted from a submitted biometric sample to those of one or more reference templates in a database and generating a resulting similarity score for each template comparison

- Decision – The determination of a match/non-match conclusion shall be based on the similarity score(s) meeting or exceeding a specified threshold or more complex decision processing such as multi-biometric fusion or candidate lists.

The decision task should be further interpreted in an application dependent manner. Resulting actions may include one or both of the following decision processes:

- Application Level Decision - The result of the search may automatically:
  - generate one or more predetermined messages to the operator of the device
  - trigger an alert (to one or more other systems or operators)
  - initiate a search or retrieve additional data from one or more other systems (e.g. intelligence systems, facial image databases etc)
  - be passed to a human operator for manual verification
  - be returned as 'raw' image data to the operator of the mobile device

  Note: An application level decision may take place on either or both sides of any network (e.g. centrally at an ABIS or locally on the device itself).

- Operator Decision - Depending on the specific application and the result of the search, the operator of the mobile device may or may not be free to make his or her own decision on how to proceed in a particular case
  - In some scenarios specific instructions such as 'arrest this person', 'do not detain this person', 'this is the same person as their supplied credential indicates', or 'this is not the same person as their supplied credential indicates' may be returned
  - In other cases the result of the search, possibly together with demographic or other metadata, or including one or more facial images of the potential 'matches' may be returned to assist the operator in deciding what action to take.

The primary tasks of image capture, image processing, matching, and output decision generation can be performed by the capture device alone or by splitting the workload with a networked system. Factors influencing the operation of these functions include location, availability of network connectivity, bandwidth of the network connection and interoperability with other systems. The cloud in Figure 1 represents a network connection. The (a) portion of the figure illustrates a standalone approach where the biometric Mobile ID capture device performs all four functions. The remaining three parts of the figure illustrate varying degrees of task allocation across a networked system.

Figure 1 Tasks Across 4 Basic Scenarios

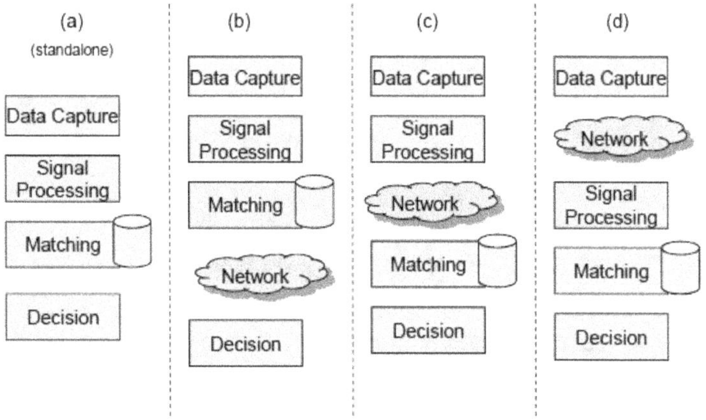

Other tasks to be performed, but not illustrated, include the addition of contextual data, the formatting of the data (to the ANSI/NIST-ITL 1-2007, the FBI EBTS, the DoD EBTS, or another standard format), and the handling of transactions and responses.

There are also administrative tasks that may need to be accomplished. They include, configuring the device for a particular scenario, the loading/updating of watch-lists, actions to be taken by the operator in different situations, logging of encounters, output of log files and other metrics, etc.

The requirements of the application for the mobile system drive the system architecture and the requirements of the individual components of that system.

5.2   Physical

The physical instantiation of the mobile system also impacts system requirements. Physical considerations include:
- how system components are connected (or not)
- connectivity to other systems (sharing/interoperability)
- security aspects of interconnected components

A physical instantiation might include one or more of the following:
- handheld biometric sensors
- handheld data entry devices
- handheld communications to a central location
- handheld communications to nearby vehicle
- vehicle based data entry
- vehicle based communications to a central location

A biometric sensor can either be a peripheral (wired or wireless) device or integrated into a mobile ID device. As indicated in Figure 1, there are many different solutions that may work depending on the needs of individual workflows. Consider these four basic concepts:
- Capture and transmit to a PC
- Capture and transmit to a PC and receive response for notification to the operator
- Capture and transmit directly to the backend system, then receive response for notification to the operator
- Capture, process (including matching), and respond to the operator.

A mobile ID device can be implemented either as a self contained unit (a single box) with the communications embedded in the device, as a peripheral or as a set of interconnected peripherals, each with its own function.

5.3   Data Format

The mobile system architecture is also closely tied with the data formats. Typical data format considerations include:
- format in transport, both for transmitting and for receiving data
- format at exposed interfaces
- data compression
- packet size (related to radio transport)
- network bandwidth, latency
- storage space (of processed or raw data)
- data security for storage and transmission
- data secrecy and data authentication.

6   Mobile ID Fingerprint Capture Devices

6.1   Overview

The capture of a high quality fingerprint enrollment image is critical. It is the sample against which other captured verification or identification samples will be compared. Unacceptable matcher performance due to poor quality stored enrollment images cannot be fixed short of acquiring a new enrollment image. Table 1, divided into capture, and interchange categories lists the sets of minimum requirements by SAP level for fingerprint capture devices. The enrollment function should be concerned with acquiring one or more very high quality images. For that reason, images captured with an NFIQ value of 4 or 5 should not normally be used for enrollment purposes. After a very high quality enrollment image has been acquired and stored, images for verification and identification comparisons may be of lower image quality.

It is up to the system designer of each particular application to determine the appropriate SAP levels for each of the enrollment, identification, or verification functions especially if there is an intention to exchange data with other systems. Captured images containing more than a single finger must use the ANSI/NIST Type-14 record in order to specify the segmentation coordinates for each finger.

The best practice recommendation is that an initial image quality assessment should be done to provide feedback to the operator during the capture process. In most cases, this function is best located on the device, although further quality assessment may also take place elsewhere in the system. The system should use the NFIQ algorithm and should alert the operator if a poor fingerprint image was captured (NFIQ level 4 or 5.)

6.1.1 Current Technology for Mobile ID Fingerprint Devices

Recommendations described in this document are applicable to current and future operational fingerprint systems and devices. For improved interoperability across dissimilar AFISs, the mobile device needs to correctly capture, compress and transmit the fingerprint images. Careful consideration and compliance to these key criteria can ensure a successful degree of interoperability and verification or identification accuracy using mobile fingerprint capture devices.

Table 1 - Fingerprint image capture device requirements

Capture[3]	SAP Level							
	5	10	20	30	40	45	50	60
Acquire flat images	Yes	Yes	Yes	Yes	Yes	Yes	Yes	Yes
Acquire rolled images	No	No	No	No	Optional	Optional	Optional	Optional
Minimum resolution	500 ppi ± 10 ppi	500 ppi ± 10 ppi	500 ppi ± 10 ppi	500 ppi ± 10 ppi	500 ppi ±10 ppi [4]	500 ppi ± 5 ppi	500 ppi ± 5 ppi	500 ppi ± 5 ppi
Minimum Gray levels	256	256	256	256	256	256	256	256
Minimum Image Dimensions (wxh)	.5" x .65"	.5" x .65"	.6" x .8"	.8" x 1.0"	1.6" x 1.5"	1.6" x 1.5"	2.5" x 1.5"	3.2" x 3"
Minimum image area	.325 sq in	.325 sq in	.48 sq in	.8 sq in	2.4 sq in	2.4 sq in	3.75 sq in	9.6 sq in
Compression algorithm[5]	N/A	WSQ	WSQ	WSQ	WSQ	WSQ	WSQ	WSQ
Maximum compression ratio	N/A	10:1	10:1	10:1	15:1	15:1	15:1	15:1
Simultaneous number of fingers	1	1	1	1	1 to 2	1 to 2	1 to 3	1 to 4
Sensor certification	PIV	PIV	PIV	PIV	PIV	Appendix F	Appendix F	Appendix F
Minutiae extractor certification	PIV	N/A	N/A	N/A	N/A	N/A	N/A	N/A
Interchange								
Image / template	Minutiae	Image	Image	Image	Image	Image	Image	Image
Standard used	INCITS 378-2004	ANSI/ NIST Type-4 or Type-14	ANSI/ NIST Type-4 or Type-14	ANSI/ NIST Type-4 or Type-14	ANSI/ NIST Type-4 or Type-14	ANSI/ NIST Type-4 or Type-14	ANSI/ NIST Type-4 or Type-14	ANSI/ NIST Type-4 or Type-14

---

[3] Scanner resolutions values specified in pixels per inch (ppi) as well as scanner platen dimensions and capture area sizes specified in inches are based on widely used specification guidelines for such devices and is accepted as common nomenclature within the industry. SI units for these will not be presented in this document for these values.

[4] SAP levels 40 and 45 are the same with the exception of the tolerance applied to minimum resolution and the required certification. Level 40 uses a 2% tolerance for minimum resolution in accordance with the PIV specification. Level 45 only provides for a 1% tolerance in accordance with the ANSI/NIST standard. Level 45 also meets the more stringent image quality conditions in EBTS Appendix F.

[5] See section 6.2.4 for information regarding increased compression ratio for levels 40 and above.

6.1.2 Quantity of Biometric Data

The number of fingers used and the amount of data captured for each finger significantly affects the overall system accuracy.

- Best practices recommend that mobile devices are configurable so that they can capture the specified fingers for a particular application.
- The number of fingers to be used depends on the Use case (see Table 6).
- When fewer than 10 fingerprints are being captured for interoperability across dissimilar systems, it is recommended that fingers 2, 3, 7, & 8 be used.
- Tests have shown that using 4 fingers rather than 2 results in a significant improvement in accuracy, even though a minimum specification calls for the use of two index fingers.
- The middle finger is also effective in matching and the middle-index pair will transition to two finger systems in the future.
- Enrollments for a system that supports latent searches should include thumbs.
- Images that are not large enough to contain the complete fingerprint may reduce the accuracy.

6.1.3 Finger Position

Within a record, the finger position number code shall be an entry chosen from the Finger Position Code table of the ANSI/NIST-ITL standard. For convenience, the appropriate finger codes are reproduced below in Table 2 together with codes for common simultaneous 2-finger and 3-finger combinations.

Table 2 - Finger position codes for single and combinations of fingers

Finger Position	Finger Code	Finger Position	Finger Code
Unknown	0	Right index & middle	40
Right thumb	1	Right middle & ring	41
Right index	2	Right ring & little	42
Right middle	3	Left index & middle	43
Right ring	4	Left middle & ring	44
Right little	5	Left ring & little	45
Left thumb	6	Right & left index	46
Left index	7	Right index, middle & ring	47
Left middle	8	Right middle, ring, & little	48
Left ring	9	Left index, middle, & ring	49
Left little	10	Left middle, ring, and little	50
Plain right thumb	11		
Plain left thumb	12		
Plain right four fingers	13		
Plain left four fingers	14		
Left & right plain thumbs	15		

6.1.4 Sequence Errors

Fingerprint images with finger numbers mislabeled will result in lower identification and verification accuracy. Fingers captured one at a time have a tendency for sequence errors. Systems with high accuracy requirements will need to search the captured fingers in multiple combinations.

6.2 Fingerprint Capture Requirements

6.2.1 Minimum Resolution

The minimum acceptable scanning resolution is 500 ppi with a tolerance of ± 5 ppi for EBTS Appendix F compliance or ± 10 ppi for PIV compliance. Scanning resolutions greater than this may be used according to guidance by the specific use cases and system(s) that interoperability is being planned for.

6.2.2 Minimum Image Dimensions (WxH)

The minimum acceptable dimensions for a fingerprint image shall be 0.5" x 0.65" which computes to a minimum area of 0.325 in^2. These dimensions can only be used to accommodate a partial flat impression. The legacy rolled fingerprint image with dimensions of 1.6"x1.5" and an area of 2.4 in^2 is captured using an SAP of 45 and meets the quality requirements of Appendix F. An SAP of 40 captures the same sized image at slightly reduced (PIV) quality. As the SAP level increases so does the overall size of the image and number of fingers which can be simultaneously captured.

6.2.3 Compression Algorithm

All captured fingerprint images shall use the WSQ algorithm to compress the 500 ppi images before being transmitted. Images scanned at 1000 ppi and compressed using the JPEG 2000 algorithm, will use the Profile for 1000 ppi Fingerprint Compression[6] to transcode these images to 500 ppi WSQ files for transmission to networked systems that require 500 ppi imagery compressed with WSQ.

6.2.4 Compression Ratio

For small area images captured at SAP levels of 10, 20, and 30 the maximum compression ratio to be used is 10:1. For larger area captured at SAP of 40 or higher the compression ratio may increase to an average of 15:1. These limits also apply to those images scanned at 1000 ppi and transcoded down to 500 ppi. The increase in the maximum allowable compression ratio when progressing from SAP 30 to SAP 40 should not be viewed as a decrease in requirement stringency.

---

[6] http://www.mitre.org/work/tech_papers/tech_papers_04/lepley_fingerprint/lepley_fingerprint.pdf

6.2.5 Sensor Certification

Sensors used to acquire images for SAP levels 45 and above shall have the current EBTS Appendix F, IAFIS Image Quality Specifications certification [7]. Smaller sensors with SAP levels of 40 and below shall have the PIV Image Quality Specifications for Single Finger Capture Devices certification[8].

6.2.6 Minutiae Extractor Certification

The SAP level 5 is the level used for the exchange of minutiae extracted from an image. When this mode is used, the minutia extractor shall be one that has been certified by NIST as being PIV compliant and interoperable with other templates and systems. These extractors were certified as a result of the MINEX interoperability tests.

6.3   Fingerprint Interchange Requirements

6.3.1 Image vs. Template

To support interoperability between systems without sacrificing search accuracy the preferred approach to fingerprint based mobile identification is to transmit the finger image(s), thereby enabling the finger minutiae to be extracted and processed on the system where the matching will actually take place.

However there are some cases where a minutiae based approach may be acceptable (e.g. if the device is only used in conjunction with a single algorithm or system) or where the transmission of images may not be possible (due to network bandwidth limitations for example).

Mobile ID devices may also be used to verify a person's identity against an ID card or token on which a biometric is stored, and such data may be either image or minutia based.

The SAP level 5 is the level used for the exchange of minutiae extracted from an image. Regardless of the size of the image captured, only SAP level 5 can be used to exchange minutiae, in lieu of exchanging the image itself.

---

[7] http://www.fbibiospecs.org/fbibiometric/ebts.html
[8] http://www.fbibiospecs.org/fbibiometric/docs/pivspec.pdf

6.3.2 Standard Used

For the exchange of SAP level 5 minutiae data, the INCITS 378-2004 minutiae data format standard developed by the M1 committee shall be used. For all other SAP levels, the ANSI/NIST-ITL 1-2007 data interchange format standard shall be used to encode image files and other metadata.

For the exchange of SAP level 10-or-higher image data, please refer to Sections 6.2.3 and 6.2.4 of this document for guidance on image compression. Additional guidance is available in Section 5.6 of the ANSI/NIST-ITL 1-2007 as well as Section 3.9.2 of the EBTS, Version 8.1 standard in cases where data exchange with the FBI is needed.

In order to promote interoperability between systems, the best practice recommendation is that the Type-14 logical record shall be used for flat or rolled impressions at 500ppi WSQ or 1000ppi (transcoded down to 500 ppi WSQ), and the Type-4 should only be used rolled 500ppi WSQ compressed images. However, the record type to be used for either flat or rolled images is dependent on the transaction type, the capabilities, and the protocols of the receiving system. The sender of the transaction must coordinate with the recipient systems in order to determine whether Type-4 or Type-14 is appropriate for a particular transaction type and for that system. Additional considerations are also required for transactions being sent to older legacy systems or a cascaded submission line.

7 Mobile ID Facial Image Capture Devices

7.1 Overview

Facial images can be used in situations where fingerprints cannot be taken. Capturing facial images provides a non-contact form of identification/verification for situations where physical contact may not be possible or practical for whatever reason. Capture of facial images can be done at a distance and therefore provides the capability for covert mobile identification operations. Capturing facial images may be of more value than taking fingerprints in some circumstances. For example, known or suspected terrorist databases or other watch lists may be more likely to contain facial images than fingerprints.

Mobile ID devices may provide the functionality for capturing and/or displaying facial images for two distinct purposes:

- Verification (e.g. for manual corroboration of a proposed identification made through a fingerprint search of a low-quality submitted image)
    - Low-resolution cameras with fixed focal length provide sufficient data for linking the return information to the subject.
    - Video acquisition is acceptable if a single frame is used, as if captured by a digital still camera.

- Identification (using the facial image to search against a database of other facial images)
    - Mobile identification using facial recognition requires higher end camera features.
    - Video acquisition is acceptable if a single frame is used, as if captured by a digital still camera.

The ANSI/NIST-ITL 1-2007 standard identifies a field [10.013] to register the Subject Acquisition profile (SAP). This is used to *"provide a general description of the criteria under which the facial image was captured."* The possible values for this field are listed in Table 18 of the ANSI/NIST standard. Section 15 of the standard provides a brief description for each of these values. The standard also states that for SAP values of 40 or greater used in field 10.013, field 10.023 becomes mandatory. This second field provides acquisition source codes – listed in Table 21 of the standard. Many other optional fields, including eye color and hair color, become mandatory for SAP levels of 40 or higher SAP.

SAP levels of 40 or higher require performance that is not easily achieved with a hand held device. The relative centering error and the 18% gray backdrop with appropriate lighting are two such considerations affecting performance. Therefore these best practice recommendations do not include full SAP compliance per the ANSI/NIST standard. Note that the standard also has an informative Appendix I, Best Practice Image Capture Requirements for SAP Levels 40, 50, and 51. Again we are not recommending that all of these best practices are applicable to mobile devices. A good example is that the standard recommends 5 facial images for SAP levels 50 and 51. There are very specific roll, yaw, and pitch angles specified. It is unlikely that they can be achieved at the side of the road without taking too long for successful acquisition.

So we see that there is a set of standards for the facial image SAP levels and a set of recommendations for implementing them – both in the ANSI/NIST standard. To supplement them for mobile ID applications, this informative best practice adds yet a third set of factors to consider. Only the actual normative standard is mandatory and only to the extent specified in the standard. The appropriate fields from the standard are listed in Table 3. Note that there are other mandatory fields such as vertical and horizontal line length that are mandatory – they are not included here because they are insensitive to SAP levels.

Table 3 - Required ANSI/NIST Type-10 fields

Ident	Condition Code	Condition Test	Field Number	Field Name
SAP	M		10.013	Subject acquisition profile
POS	O	Mandatory for facial images	10.020	Subject pose
POA	O	Mandatory if Field 10.20 has an A value	10.021	Pose offset angle
PAS	O	Mandatory if SAP has a value of 40 or higher	10.023	Photo acquisition source
SXS	O	Mandatory if SAP has a value of 40 or higher	10.026	Subject facial description [see Table 22 in the standard]
SEC	O	Mandatory if SAP has a value of 40 or higher	10.027	Subject eye color [see Table 23 in the standard]
SHC	O	Mandatory if SAP has a value of 40 or higher	10.028	Subject hair color [see Table 24 in the standard]

Table 4 lists the sets of minimum requirements recommended for SAP levels 32, 42, and 52.[9] for facial image capture appropriate for Mobile ID devices per the ANSI/NIST standard. In order to avoid confusion, these levels are analogous to the recommended SAP levels 30, 40, and 51 definitions contained in the best practice Appendix I of the ANSI/NIST standard.

The table is divided into capture and interchange requirements. It is up to the system designer of each particular application to determine the appropriate SAP levels for each of the enrollment, identification, or verification functions especially if there is an intention to exchange data with other systems.

The Mobile ID face capture device must be able to either measure the face image quality or provide some means by which the device operator can subjectively assess the quality of the captured face image. The best practice recommendation is that an initial image quality assessment should be done to provide feedback to the operator during the capture process. In most cases, this function is best located on the device, although further quality assessment may also take place elsewhere in the system. However, no standardized quality algorithm is broadly available that would aid system interoperability. The device should alert the operator if the captured face image is of insufficient quality.

---

[9] SAP levels of 13, 14, and 15 can be considered for local use, for instance when verifying against an ID card that has an imbedded facial image on a chip or on an RFID tag.

7.2   Face Capture Requirements

7.2.1 Capture Distance

Cameras using facial recognition for mobile identification need a focal length that is compatible with 60 – 200 cm (~2-6 feet) of separation between the device and the subject. Self-images of the operator, intended for operator authentication, audit trail, calibration, etc., require images taken at approximately two feet from the operator. Separation between the operator and the subject is typically 100 to 200 cm (~3-6 feet).

7.2.2 Capture Device Controls

Camera controls enable the camera, with assistance from the operator or automatically (if set on auto), to capture quality pictures in bright sunlight, overcast light, indoors, or using additional lighting at night.

7.2.3 Capture Device Frame Rate

Image display of 15 frames per second is approximately real time for viewing while the operator frames the facial image properly using the camera display. However, a 12 frames per second rate is adequate for any of the SAP listed in
Table 4. Automated facial detection frame rates are typically 5-10 frames per second. High-end digital cameras refresh the on-board camera display at a rate of about a 6-7 frames per second.

7.2.4 Photo Image Format

Images are captured at a minimum of in 24-bit RGB or 8-bit monochrome and in a format compatible with NIST Best Practices, Appendix I. For facial recognition, color images should be used.

7.2.5 Capture Device Image Size and Aspect Ratio

Image sizes are linked to the ANSI/NIST-ITL 1-2007 specifications in Appendix I for image size.

7.2.6 Capture Device Sensitivity

Cameras with sensitivity to 4 lux provide images sufficient for associating returns in marginal lighting conditions. Images taken under such lighting conditions will not normally be of sufficient quality for automated facial recognition.

7.2.7 Facial Image Compression

Facial image compression shall be done in accordance with clauses 5.6.1, 15.1.11, and 15.1.36 of the ANSI/NIST-ITL 1-2007 Standard.

7.3   Standard Used

For the exchange of facial images at all of the SAP levels, the ANSI/NIST-ITL 1-2007 data interchange format standard Type-10 logical record shall be used to encode compressed image files and other metadata.

Table 4 - Facial image capture device requirements

Capture	ANSI/NIST Comments	Levels		
		32	**42**	**52**
Image resolution (size)	Lower resolution may reduce accuracy	≥ 480x600	≥ 768x1024	≥ 2400x3200
Capture device sensor		Progressive scan (no interlace)	Progressive scan (no interlace)	Progressive scan (no interlace)
Capture device color space		Minimum of 24-bit RGB color space or a minimum of 8-bit monochrome color space	Minimum of 24-bit RGB color space or a minimum of 8-bit monochrome color space	Minimum of 36-bit RGB color space or a minimum of 12-bit monochrome color space
Capture device controls		Auto gain and auto shutter, optional: control loop for camera parameter (shutter speed/ flash intensity) based on face area on-board	Auto gain and auto shutter, optional: control loop for camera parameter (shutter speed/ flash intensity) based on face area on-board (requires continuous face detection)	Auto gain and auto shutter, optional: control loop for camera parameter (shutter speed/ flash intensity) based on face area on-board (requires continuous face detection)
Capture distance in mm	Lower distance may reduce accuracy	60-200 cm (~ 2-6 feet), the longer distance is preferred	60-200 cm, the longer distance is preferred	60-200 cm, the longer distance is preferred
Illuminator type – optional feature		Xenon flash or LED / fill in flash	Xenon flash or LED / fill in flash	Xenon flash or LED / fill in flash
Ambient light[10]	Minimum light level at which flash becomes required	4 lux	4 lux	4 lux
Wavelength range		Visible light, 380-780nm	Visible light, 380-780nm	Visible light, 380-780nm
Exposure time	Capability to freeze motion	≤ 1/100s (10 ms)	≤ 1/100s (10 ms)	≤ 1/100s (10 ms)
Inter-eye distance	Lower resolution may reduce accuracy	≥ 90pixels	≥ 150pixels	≥ 300pixels
Frame rate	For positioning (live view)	≥ 12 fps	≥ 12 fps	≥ 12 fps
Interchange				
Format		ANSI/NIST-ITL Type-10	ANSI/NIST-ITL Type-10	ANSI/NIST-ITL Type-10

---

[10] These values do not factor in light intensifier technology.

8 Mobile ID Iris Image Capture Devices

8.1 Overview

Table 5 lists the sets of minimum requirements for SAP level 20, 30 & 40 for Mobile ID iris image capture devices. The table is divided into capture and interchange portions. It is up to the system designer of each particular application to determine the appropriate SAP levels for each of the enrollment, identification, or verification functions especially if there is an intention to exchange data with other systems.

The Mobile ID iris capture device must be able to measure the iris image quality. The best practice recommendation is that an initial image quality assessment should be done to provide feedback to the operator during the capture process. In most cases, this function is best located on the device, although further quality assessment may also take place elsewhere in the system. However, no standardized quality algorithm is broadly available that would aid system interoperability. The device should alert the operator if the captured iris image is of insufficient quality.

8.2 Capture Requirements

8.2.1 Iris Diameter in True Pixels

The minimum acceptable iris image diameter is 140 true, non-up-sampled pixels. This value increases with the SAP level up to 210 pixels.

8.2.2 Number of Simultaneously or Quasi-simultaneously Captured Irises

Some iris imagers are capable of capturing both left and right iris images simultaneously or quasi-simultaneously (within a few milliseconds). The lower SAP level devices may only be required to capture one iris at a time, but at SAP 42, the minimum requirement is that both iris images be simultaneously captured. This feature assures the correct assignment of left-right for each image. It also allows for more accurate estimation of the roll angle and potentially higher accuracy and comparison speed.

8.2.3 Exposure Time

The ability for an iris image capture device to suppress motion blur and to freeze motion, is a function of exposure time. The maximum allowable value for the exposure time, expressed in milliseconds, reduces as SAP levels increase, from a maximum of 33 ms.

8.2.4 Viewfinder and Image Quality Feedback

Mobile iris capture devices can be configured differently with regard to the operator interface, in terms of the viewfinder (being external or internal) and the manner of providing image quality feedback to the operator. These factors will influence the rate of successful captures. As SAP level increases, the complexity / sophistication of the feedback mechanisms increases.

8.2.5 Capture Distance

In order to be considered acceptable as non-intrusive and to avoid excessive geometric distortion, the minimum distance between the mobile iris capture device's lens and the subject's eye must be at least 100 millimeters.

8.2.6 Capture Volume

In order to provide an acceptable level of usability and ease of alignment, the camera must allow for some variability in the position of the iris center relative to the camera. This variability is defined by position tolerances in the horizontal, vertical, and axial dimensions that together define a volume (the "capture volume") within which the center of the iris must be located in order to enable image capture. For devices that do not utilize mechanical alignment aids, the capture volume should be at least 11 mm wide, 9 mm high, and 20 mm deep. For devices that do possess a mechanical alignment aid, such as a visor or head rest, the capture volume should be at least 11 mm wide, 9 mm high, and 12 mm deep. Devices that capture both eyes without repositioning between captures must have a wider capture volume to accommodate variation in inter-pupillary distance (IPD). In this case the capture volume dimensions for devices without mechanical alignment aids are 19 mm wide, 14 mm high, and 20 mm deep, and for devices with such aids, 19 mm wide, 14 mm high, and 12 mm deep.

8.2.7 Imaging Wavelength Range and Spectral Spread

The iris imaging device must be capable of capturing light in the range of 700-900 nanometers. The camera's near infrared illuminator(s) must have a controlled spectral content, such that the overall spectral imaging sensitivity, including the sensor characteristics, transfers at least 35% of the power per any 100nm-wide sub-band of the 700-900nm range.

8.2.8 Scan Type

The iris capture sensor shall use progressive scanning.

8.2.9 Image Margins in Pixels Around Iris Border

In order to retain sufficient image surrounding of the iris, for the purpose of identifying the left or right eye as well as for a more accurate iris segmentation, the margins around the iris portion of the image need to be at least 50% of the iris diameter on the left and right sides of the image, and a least 25% of the iris diameter on the top and bottom of the image.

8.2.10   Image Evaluation Frame Rate

In order to achieve acceptable time-to-capture and FTA rates, the iris image sampling frequency must be at least 5 frames per second.

Table 5 - Iris image capture requirements

Capture	Affects	Levels		
		20	**30**	**40**
Iris diameter in true, non-up-sampled pixels	Accuracy	≥140 pixel	≥170 pixel	≥210 pixel
Number of (quasi-) simultaneously captured eyes	Capture speed, search speed, accuracy	≥1	≥1	2
Exposure time	Capability to freeze motion	≤33 ms	≤15 ms	≤10 ms
Viewfinder & Image quality feedback	Rate of successful captures	External or Internal	Internal, Optical or electronic	Internal, At least electronic
Capture distance in mm	Intrusiveness, operator safety	≥100		
Capture volume per eye, minimum width / height / depth in mm	Ease of alignment	Regular devices: 11mm / 9mm / 20mm for single-eye capture 19mm / 14mm / 20mm for two-eye capture Device with a mechanical alignment aid: 11mm / 9mm / 12mm for single-eye capture 19mm / 14mm / 12mm for two-eye capture		
Imaging wavelength range and spectral spread	Dependence of accuracy on eye color	700-900 nm Sensitivity ≥35% the power in any 100nm band		
Scan type	Accuracy, compressibility	Progressive		
Image margins in pixels around iris border	Accuracy	Left & right: 0.50 d Top & bottom: 0.25 d (d = iris diameter in pixels)		
Image evaluation frame rate	Time to capture and failure to acquire	≥5 frames/s		
Allowable maximum average irradiance	Relevant for eye safety	Governed by Iec 825-1 and iso 60825-1		
Sensor signal-to-noise ratio	Recognition accuracy	≥36db		
Interchange				
Pixel depth in 700-900 nm range	Interoperability	≥8 bits/pixel		
Format, iris	Interoperability	Raw Iso 19794-6-rectilinear ANSI/NIST type-17		

8.2.11   Allowable Maximum Average Irradiance

Mobile Identification devices using iris image capture typically provide infrared lighting using LEDs to illuminate the iris. The illumination is in a range partly visible to the human eye. Illumination shall be compliant with illumination standard IEC 825-1 and safety specification ISO 60825-1.

8.2.12   Sensor Signal-to-noise Ratio

In order to achieve acceptable recognition accuracy, the iris acquisition sensor must achieve a signal-to-noise ration of at least 36dB.

8.3   Iris Interchange Requirements

8.3.1 Pixel Depth in 700-900 nm Range

Within the frequency range of interest, 700-900 nm, the iris sensor must generate images with at least 8 bits per pixel.

8.3.2 Format

In order to support interoperability, the mobile iris capture device must support ANSI.NIST Type-17 records, with raw images conformant to ISO 19794-6 rectilinear image standards.

8.3.3 Iris-specific Peak Signal-to-noise Ratio Due to JPEG/JPEG2K Compression

When iris images are subjected to JPEG or JPEG2000 compression, the peak signal-to-noise ratio shall be at least the level as determined by the NIST IREX evaluation.

9   Mobile ID Use Cases

9.1   Overview

For handheld Mobile ID devices, Table 6 lists mobile identification use cases applicable to fingerprints, face, and iris. Ten different scenarios have been defined based on risk levels to public safety and also on the intended function. Risk levels are summarized as severe, moderate, and mild. Each risk level has specific implications for image quality requirements of the three biometric functions: enrollment, identification, and verification.

The Use Cases listed Table 6 indicate aggressive image size and quality requirements needed to meet the severe security risk levels, independent of technology availability. Devices meeting these requirements may not be currently available in the mobile identification market but projections indicate that devices meeting these criteria will be available in the 2010-2015 timeframe based on current R&D efforts.

9.2   Severe Risk Environments

Severe risk levels imply that loss of life and/or property can result if accurate identification or verification is not made. In severe risk environments, it is plausible that inconvenience to the subject being identified or verified is secondary to the security of the situation, meaning subjects may be detained longer until the identification or verification process is completed. This assumption means that ABIS or other matching thresholds can be set lower (more aggressively) resulting in a returned list of potential candidates that a forensics examiner may review to determine if a true match has occurred. With the ability to have a forensics examiner review the images, image quality meeting the stringent FBI IAFIS IQS Appendix F requirements[11] or other quality criteria adds information that can be used by the examiner. A forensics fingerprint examiner can use level 3 fingerprint information including inter-ridge detail and pore structure to effect identifications. On the other hand, machine matching is typically constrained to level 2 minutiae details and ridge spacing. For this reason, fingerprint sensors for enrollment and identification in a severe environment must meet Appendix F Image Quality Specifications. In addition, each print that can be compared adds information that can be used by the examiner making full ten-print comparisons desirable.

Examples of enrollment and identification functions in a high risk environment include background checks conducted to grant access to secure facilities during battle field operations. In this case, enrollment fingerprints would be compared against the latent image database maintained by the Department of Defense (DoD). Applying requirements for FBI Appendix F IQS maximizes the likelihood of obtaining a match against the latent database.

The verification function typically compares a processed captured biometric image against previously captured templates. Thus, even for verification functions performed in a severe risk environment, sensors meeting PIV image quality specifications provide the maximum data that will be used for matching. Increased confidence for verification functions can be met using multi-instance (e.g. 2 or more fingers) or multi-modal biometric verification. This approach has been applied by the US military in granting access cards to citizens for access to villages in Iraq and Afghanistan.

9.3   Moderate Risk Environments

A moderate risk environment is defined for those encounters with a subject with no or questionable identification. An officer cannot detain a subject for more than a limited amount of time without making an arrest. In this situation, it is necessary to quickly identify the subject or retain biometric information sufficient to verify the subject's identity at a later date. In these situations PIV image quality enables machine matching of images. In the event these prints are enrolled, these images are sufficient to match the subject when they are later encountered in the court system. Once the subject is in the court system, any images retained using mobile enrollment would typically be replaced by images captured using a ten-print system. Once again, the capture of more images provides more information for later booking. In addition, the capture of two or more fingerprints simultaneously provides additional information on the fingerprint sequence.

---

[11] At this time there is no commonly acknowledged equivalent image quality specifications for either face or iris capture devices.

Table 6 - Use cases for risks and functions

Risk to Public Safety/Function	Use Case Example	SAP Level			Notes
		Face	Finger	Iris	
Severe/ Enrollment	Field enrollment into databases with applications where there is a high risk of loss of life or assets. Some situations may require multi-modal biometric enrollment. Enrollment should achieve an equivalent level of quality as if conducted in a controlled environment using non-mobile devices.	42	45+	40	Recommend Capture: Iris = L&R Finger = 10 Enrolling all ten fingerprints, multiple views faces including full-face with three to five profiles, both irises, and multiple instances (captures) of each biometric provides additional search capabilities. Note for face enrollments, attempts should be made to control, background expression and lighting where it is practical to do so.
Severe/ Identification	One to many search against a database to identify a subject where there is a high risk of loss of life or assets. Some situations may require multi-modal biometric identification.	42	45+	40	Recommend Capture: Iris = L&R eyes Finger = 4+ Note for face identifications, attempts should be made to control, background expression and lighting where it is practical to do so.
Severe/ Verification	1:1 match against a credential or database to verify identity where there is a high risk of loss of life or assets. Some situations may require multi-modal biometric verification.	32+	20+	40	Recommend Capture: Iris = Either eye Finger = 2+ Note for face verifications, attempts should be made to control, background expression and lighting where it is practical to do so.
Moderate/ Enrollment	Mobile booking: Field cite and release when the violation is not high enough to ensure incarceration until arraignment without bail.	42	40+	30	Recommend Capture: Iris = L&R eyes Finger = 6+ Note for face enrollments and identifications, ideal lighting conditions should be used. Otherwise, fingerprints or irises should additionally be used.
Moderate/ Identification	In field mobile identification of a subject with questionable or no identification.	42	30+	30	Recommend Capture: Iris = Either eye Finger = 4+
Moderate/ Verification	Personal Identity Verification (PIV) Release from custody.	32+	20+	30	Recommend Capture: Iris = Either eye Finger = 2+
Mild/ Enrollment	The intention is for the biometric enrollment to be of sufficient quality that it shall allow later verification (e.g. e-citations).	32	30+	20	Recommend Capture: Iris = L&R eye Finger = 4+
Mild /Identification	Rapid identification in custody prior to formal booking. (Typically done at the jail intake.)	32	10+	20	Recommend Capture: Iris = Either eye Finger = 2+
Mild/ Verification (finger images).	Court Appearance/Parole/Workhouse, Personal Identity Verification (PIV).	22+	10+	20	Recommend Capture: Iris = Either eye Finger = 1+
Mild/ Verification (finger minutiae).	Personal Identity Verification (PIV) (using minutiae).	N/A	5+	N/A	Recommend Capture: Finger = 2+ Not recommended for use between AFIS.

Requirements for verification functions in these environments often match those of the high risk environment since machine matching is used against previously captured templates. PIV image quality meets the criteria required for verification in these environments.

9.4 Mild Risk Environments

A mild risk environment is defined for those encounters where enrollment and identification data will be used at a later date. At that time the subject would be available for comparison to the data previously retained. The results of an identification or verification should not impact anyone but the subject in question. Examples of mild enrollments include preparing for future logical or physical access control for a subject, or retaining one or more biometric images for verification in court while the subject is available. Verification examples include tracking a subject through the jail or court system using the retained biometric images. In these cases a failure to match would result in additional action to verify the subject's identity, primarily inconveniencing no one but the subject.

10 Transactions and Replies

Mobile ID devices are just one source of biometric-based search transactions. Just like other transactions from booking stations, etc., all such transactions must be formulated to be compliant with the ANSI/NIST-ITL 1-2007 requirements, regarding formats and encoding, and also with the target system's domain specific requirements. These requirements are typically documented in a domain-specific electronic biometric transmission specification that will also include acquisition profiles and transaction submission and security. Returned responses must also be in compliance with ANSI/NIST-ITL 1-2007 record types and the domain-specific specifications.

Transactions originating at Mobile ID devices can be part of a variety of scenarios that rely on enrollment, identification or verification of subjects. Because of the basic portability of these devices coupled with the fact that they are often used in less controlled situations than at a police station, the urgency of an identity check often dictates a quick biometric capture with the expectation of a fairly rapid response turnaround – similar to NCIC roadside searches and responses. Transaction types originating from Mobile ID devices will generally be one-to-many searches (identification) but will differ in response time and database files searched on a case-by-case basis.

For example, an officer may stop a vehicle for a moving violation and issue the driver a citation. There are several possible scenarios for this type of transaction:

- One or more biometric samples may be captured at this point and enrolled in the system in order to verify the subject's identity at a later time should it be necessary (warrant issued or possibility of identity theft)
- A search transaction may be triggered to enable a rapid search against special databases containing individuals of interest, including among others subjects with outstanding wants or warrants
- The same transaction can be used to search other agency databases (e.g., the FBI) for known or suspected terrorists, wanted aliens, or other international subjects identified as a threat to the United States. Such transactions should provide responses in a few seconds due to the limited nature of the searches and the risk to officer safety of dealing with such a subject in an uncontrolled environment. However, responses to these transactions may consist of limited feedback in the form of 'yes', 'no', or 'possibly'.

Another example could be the use of a Mobile ID device for the purpose of verifying an individual's identity. This can take the simplest form such as admittance to a government building or entrance into a country or a camp within a war zone.

In order to initiate a biometric-based search, a well-formed ANSI/NIST-ITL 1-2007 transaction must be submitted with the expectation of receiving a similar well-formed ANSI/NIST transaction in response. Some types of submittal transactions may result in a much longer response time due to requirements for the transmission and processing of large amounts of biometric data (for example, both irises, all 10 fingers, full and profile facial images, etc.) in addition to any required descriptors. A typical set of ANSI/NIST records comprising a submission might include:

- A single Type-1 header record comprised of mandatory and optional fields

- A single Type-2 record containing mandatory and descriptive data

- From 2 to 10 Type-4 or Type-14 flat or rolled fingerprint images

- From 1 to 5 Type-10 facial images (or SMTs)

- From 1 to 2 Type-17 iris images

Biometric-specific characteristics will be automatically extracted from acquired biometric images at the target system with no human intervention. These characteristics or templates are then searched against one or more databases or watch lists. When the search is completed, the results are transmitted back to the originator in response to the biometric investigative search request. If the local system communicating directly with the Mobile ID device is capable of responding in ANSI/NIST compliant record formats than that should be done. But some local business rules and existence of older, "heritage", systems might require responses in some other format. This becomes a problem for interoperability with other agencies and departments participating in major events (e.g., disaster recovery, riots, etc.) and should be avoided at all costs. The returned response should be in the form of another ANSI/NIST transaction containing at least a Type-1 and Type-2 logical record. The match report will include the identification of matching candidates and optionally the corresponding frontal facial image or matching fingerprint images of the candidate with the highest score. Often the submitter of the transaction requires these matching images for comparison and confirmation. It may also be possible to retrieve remaining candidate images through separate image retrieval requests.

11 Mobile Device Security & Encryption

11.1 Overview

The establishment and enforcement of IT and agency security policies is not the focus of this document. Law enforcement and criminal justice agencies are increasingly realizing the productivity benefits of mobile handheld devices such as PDAs and similar types of technology. Mobile ID devices represent a tremendous productivity advantage for criminal justice and ID management.

While this mobile technology and the capabilities it brings from biometric identification to citations and report writing will be a great advantage to criminal justice personnel, it is creating a tremendous security management challenge. The small size, large storage capacity and network connectivity of these devices make unprotected mobile devices susceptible to loss, theft and misuse, and possibly a target for someone wanting unauthorized access to information or databases. Mission sensitive and confidential information is now available through the mobile devices at locations and under circumstances which are outside the normal security parameters. As a result, unsecured devices can pose a risk to any criminal justice network that the device can access (for example, CJIS and NLETS). In order to adequately secure the device from misuse or attack and to meet regulatory standards and requirements, agencies must develop wireless and centralized device security policies. These policies should include measures regarding authentication, data erase, encryption, application launch controls and device feature disablement.

This best practices document is intended to establish awareness of mobile handheld security problems and to specify "best practice" counter measures to defend against these threats. In addition, this document will identify key issues that an IT security manager must address while establishing a comprehensive handheld security policy. This document will focus on security as it relates to the mobile device and the operator of that device.

FIPS 140-2 provides a great deal of information and standardization for this area, and provides a foundation for addressing this issue. The best practices references FIPS 140-2 as the primary source of a standard to be addressed for the use of handheld devices. This standard specifies the security requirements for a cryptographic module utilized within a security system protecting sensitive information in computer and telecommunication systems which addressed the functionality of the mobile devices.

The main focus of this best practices effort is on device capabilities and the ability to implement security protocols that may be specified by the various operators or agencies responsible for these handheld devices. Security policies put in place by the owner of the databases being searched must always be followed.

11.2   Data Encryption

11.2.1   FIPS 140 Standard

Although the referenced FIPS 140 standards are the ones to be used by US based agencies, agencies and organizations in other countries could require compliance to different standards that provide an equivalent level of security.

11.2.2   Transmissions

At a minimum, the data encryption algorithm used shall be AES-256. The mobile handheld device shall provide the capability for the encryption and decryption of bidirectional traffic. This should be accomplished in a manner to meet the FIPS 140-2 Type-1 requirements. Such encryption/decryption software should be FIPS 140-2 certified.

11.2.3   Data At Rest

The handheld device shall at a minimum provide the capability to encrypt all data residing on the device either as a temporary file or a part of a database in a manner to meet the FIPS 140-2 Type-1 requirements and such encryption software shall be FIPS 140-2 certified or equivalent.

11.2.4   Storage Cards

Data can be stored both in the device's RAM and in external storage cards, such as SD/MMC, CF cards and PC storage cards. Since these storage cards can save and store gigabytes of data, the mobile handheld device shall encrypt all of the device data, databases and files written to storage medium in a manner to meet the FIPS 140-2 Type-1 requirements and such encryption software shall be FIPS 140-2 certified.

11.3   Authentication and Authorization

11.3.1   Operator Authentication

The mobile handheld device should provide the capability for an operator to authenticate his/her identity as well as establishing authorization levels for that person based on a two factor authentication, one of which should be a biometric.

11.3.2   Biometric and Password

The mobile handheld device should provide biometric operator authentication and a password of minimum length with alphabetical /numeric/special characters.

11.3.3　　Re-authentication

The mobile handheld device should provide the capability for operator re-authentication after a designated length of time.

11.3.4　　Idle Time Re-authentication

The mobile handheld device should provide the capability for operator re-authentication and the device should re-authenticate itself after a designated amount of idle time or result in a device shut-off.

11.3.5　　Failed Security Protocols

The mobile handheld device should provide the capability to lock the device or render the device inoperable, erase selective files, and/or erase all files on the device based on failed security protocols.

11.3.6　　Failed Authentication Attempts

The mobile handheld device should provide the capability to establish a maximum limit of failed authentication attempts before the handheld clears all application data or requires unlock only by an IT administrator.

11.3.7　　Device Authentication

Once operator authentication and authorization is established, the mobile handheld device should be able to provide device authentication that it is authorized to communicate on the network. There should also be the capability to have the device's identification verified against an registered list of specified devices (black list, lost/stolen). A device with a matching identification to one on the list should not be authorized to communicate with the central system.

11.3.8　　Policy and Software Updates

In order to maintain the highest level of device security, an updating of all devices is needed whenever policies change or software is updated to provide greater protections. The mobile handheld device should be capable of wireless over-the-air update of device security solution.

11.3.9　　Memory Card

When inserting a protected (encrypted) memory card into the mobile handheld device's expansion slot, the device should be able to detect an encrypted card and prompt the operator for the card's authentication codes. Access to information would be granted only when the correct authentication has been provided. Encryption algorithms shall be FIPS 140-2 certified and designed to provide data encryption in a transparent method. Transparency ensures that the operator is impacted as little as possible while providing the maximum data protection.

11.3.10   Data Authentication

The data authentication algorithm used shall be RSA-2048 as defined by FIPS-186-3 2006 (DSS). The Secure Hash Function the signature will be evaluated over shall be SHA-256, as defined by FIPS-180-2. The provisioning of certificates, root certificates, and private keys shall remain outside the scope of this standard.

12 Communication Protocols

12.1 Overview

There are several different approaches for establishing communication between Mobile ID devices and systems. Figure 2 below summarizes the different approaches that can be employed.

12.2 Wireless Connectivity

Mobile ID devices that search a central database may employ a wireless connection to the central site. Wireless connectivity is dependent on local and regional capabilities. Dependent on the region of deployment, connectivity may make use of wireless technologies such as Bluetooth or Wi-Fi connections, cellular data lines, or satellite communications. Acceptable minimum data rates are dependent on the transaction size to be transmitted, reasonable limits on time of detention, and the selected communication protocol. Several different approaches will be presented in this chapter for discussion and consideration.

12.3 Cellular Connectivity

12.3.1   GSM/GPRS/EDGE/UMTS

GSM/GPRS is a pervasive 2.5G cellular technology that is widely used in Europe and Asia and by some U.S. carriers. Data rates are typically 40 kilobytes per second.

EDGE and UMTS are 3G technologies that push data rates up to 1 megabits per second.

12.3.2   CDMA/1XRTT/EVDO/EVDM

CDMA/1XRTT technology is a 2.5G technology that competes with GSM/GPRS and by some U.S. carriers. Data rates are around 40 kilobits per second.

EVDO and EVDM are 3G iterations of this technology that push data rates up to 1 megabits per second.

12.3.3   HSDPA/WCDMA

HSDPA and WCDMA represent the next phase of cellular technology and the convergence of the two technologies discussed above.   Future data rates are projected to reach 40 megabytes per second.

Figure 2 Mobile ID Communication Configuration Choices

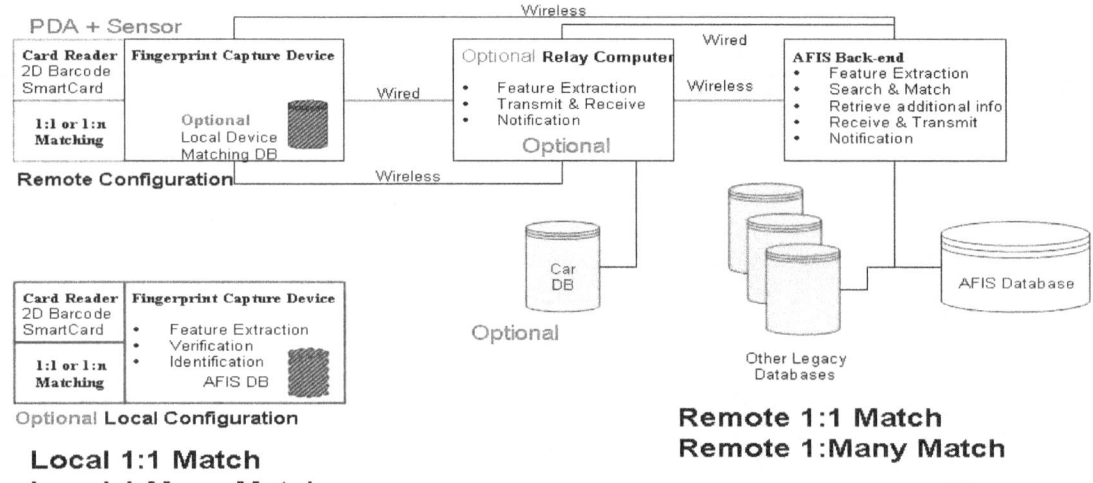

12.4 Satellite Communication

Satellite communication may be required in remote areas or at sea where other commercial communication systems are not present.   Most satellite communications require bulky transmitters/receivers.   Mobile ID devices typically communicate to these devices using cables or Bluetooth connection.

12.5 802.11b/g

Wi-Fi is a common means of wireless communication built into today's PDAs and mobile PCs. Wi-Fi communication is high speed with rates exceeding 10 megabits per second and ranges exceeding 300 meters.

12.6 Bluetooth

Bluetooth is a wireless method of connecting devices at short range.   Data rates for Bluetooth 1.0 are typically around 700 kilobits per second.   Range for Bluetooth varies based on the transmit power used.   Class 3 Bluetooth devices have a range of approximately 1 meter, class 2 approximately 10 meters, and class 1 approximately 100 meters. Bluetooth 2.0 extends the data rate of the wireless connection to three times that of Bluetooth 1.0.

12.7 Global Positioning System (GPS)

GPS functionality adds the ability for devices to location stamp transactions.

12.8 Integrated Wireless Antenna

Mobile devices include integrated antennas that support cellular connection equivalent to commercial cell phones.

12.9 Wireless Connection Status

PDA and PC applications for wireless connection provide and display the status of all wireless connections.

13 Environmental Considerations

13.1 Overview

A Mobile ID device can be used in a variety of different contexts, such as a law court, an airport terminal, by a patrol officer on the street or in a patrol car, or even in a military environment such as a checkpoint or for access control to a military base.

These different use cases each require different levels of resistance to the environmental factors such as temperature, humidity, dust, water, vibration, etc. For these reasons, three different profiles are described below (Indoor, Law Enforcement and Military), with increasing levels of resistance to the relevant environmental conditions.

It is the responsibility of the Agency to decide, in the procurement phase of the Mobile ID devices, which profile to request in the Request for Proposal (RFP). This will depend on the expected usage of the devices and the location where they will be required to operate. It is important to choose the right profile since a lower profile could mean that the devices are not able to withstand the operating environment, causing costly failures and decreasing service levels, while choosing a too high profile is likely to cause an unnecessary increase in the size, weight and cost of the devices.

13.2 Indoor Profile

If a Mobile ID device is going to be used only in an environment such as an office building, a court of law, etc. the suggested environmental specifications for the device can be assumed to be similar to those of most commercially available computing devices intended for office use. For these use cases, the recommended minimum environmental specifications are listed in Table 7.

Table 7 - Indoor Profile Recommendations

Operating temperatures	+32° +104° F 0° +40° C
Storage temperatures	+14° + 122° F -10° +50° C
Relative humidity	max. 85% non condensing
Ingress Protection Rating (IP Code)	IP 40 or higher

For more information about the level of ingress protection (IP) refer to the IEC standard 60529 "Degrees of protection provided by enclosures".

13.3 Law Enforcement Profile

This profile should be used when the Mobile ID devices are going to be used for example by a patrol officer on the street or on-board a patrol car.

These use cases require the devices to be able to withstand high or low operating temperatures, dust, rain, water splashes, the vibrations typically encountered in a vehicle and drop from a limited height. For these use cases, the recommended minimum environmental specifications are listed in Table 8.

Table 8 - Law Enforcement Profile Recommendations

Operating temperatures	+14° + 122° F -10° +50° C
Storage temperatures	-4° +140° F -20° +60° C
Relative humidity	10-90% non condensing
Ingress Protection Rating (IP Code)	IP 54 or higher, in operational configuration, with any existing expansion port closed
Drop resistance	Resistance to multiple drops on concrete from a height of 3 feet (91 cm).

13.4 Military Profile

This profile should be used when the Mobile ID devices are going to be used in harsh operating environments, when the expected use cases require the devices to provide increased level of protections against high and low temperatures, dust and sand, rain, water splashes, vibrations and drop. For these use cases, the recommended minimum environmental specifications are listed in Table 9.

If the device is going to be used in a maritime environment, an increased level of Ingress Protection should be considered, such as IP 66 (protection against water jet) or IP 67 (immersion up to 1 meter), and compliance with MIL-STD-810F Method 509.4 (Salt Fog).

Table 9 - Military Profile Recommendations

Operating temperatures	From -20°F to 140°F (-29°C to 60°C) according to MIL-STD-810F Method 501.4 Procedure II at 140°F MIL-STD-810F Method 502.4 Procedure II at -20°F
Storage temperatures	From -20°F to 140°F (-29°C to 60°C) according to MIL-STD-810F Method 501.4 Procedure I at 140°F MIL-STD-810F Method 502.4 Procedure I at -20°F
Relative humidity	MIL-STD-810F Method 507.4
Rain	MIL-STD-810F Method 506.4 Procedure I
Ingress Protection Rating (IP Code)	IP 65 or higher, in operational configuration, with any existing expansion port closed
Drop resistance	The devices should comply with MIL-STD-810F Method 516.5 – Procedure IV (Transit Drop), in non-operational configuration. If the devices do not contain a hard drive, compliance is required also in the operational configuration.
Vibration resistance	The devices should comply with MIL-STD-810F Method 514.5 – Procedure I (General Vibration), in both operational and non-operational configurations.

For additional information about the above test procedures refer to: "MIL-STD-810F - Department of Defense Test Method Standard for Environmental Engineering Considerations and Laboratory Tests", released on Jan. 1st, 2000.

14 XML Issues

All current communications with the FBI IAFIS and RISC use EFTS or EBTS formats based on the ANSI/NIST standard. Recently XML has gained wide acceptance in private and public sector applications as an effective data delivery method. The current release of ANSI/NIST-ITL 1-2007 continues the current packet format as Part 1 of the standard. The ANSI/NIST-ITL

2-2008 Part 2: XML version of the standard has now been approved. The same data elements are passed in both parts.

The ANSI/NIST-ITL 2-2008 Part 2 is based upon NIEM 2.0 (National Information Exchange Model). This model standardizes the structure and tag names for data exchanges, including criminal justice related data exchanges. The FBI has also released a DRAFT XML EBTS with interfaces compatible with ANSI/NIST-ITL 2-2008 Part 2: XML version. For new systems or those upgraded that are to be based on XML, the preference is to implement the NIEM-based ANSI/NIST-ITL 2-2008 standard.

The use of XML for the transmission of biometric data does have transmission size implications. Using the base 64 concept for encoding image data the transmission size will increase by at least 30%. Therefore, other methods may be more appropriate for those instances when bandwidth is a factor for consideration.

Annex A Mobile ID Device Features
(Informative)

A.1 General

Mobile ID devices features are driven by the application of the device. As previously stated, applications can be divided into the law enforcement, military (DoD), and civilian verification segments. Each of these segments brings specific requirements to the device feature set and should be evaluated as such. Features required for law enforcement or DoD may be different than those needed for civil verification.

A.2 Platforms

A.2.1 Processors

Standalone capture devices typically use on board Digital Signal Processors (DSP) or embedded processors (such as ARM, or Advanced RISC Machines) meant for low power applications. Operating systems are typically dedicated to the specific processor. Applications are custom to the device and are not interoperable with third party applications.

PDA based applications typically use the same embedded processors but have operating systems that enable use of third party applications. Typical operating systems are Windows (Embedded, Mobile, CE, or .NET), Linux, Palm OS, or the Symbian OS.

A.2.2 Storage capacity

Standalone capture devices typically provide storage capacity to capture multiple sets of fingerprints, faces, and or irises in an uncompressed format. Total memory required is dependent on the number of biometric samples captured and the number of subjects to be retained on the device. PDA based applications require memory for biometric applications, compression algorithms, and communications software, including encryption and security applications. Current generation PDAs typically provide 128 Megabytes of RAM, 128 megabytes of Flash, and optional flash cards with storage up to and exceeding several gigabytes of storage. Today's PC based applications typically have up to 1 gigabyte of RAM or more and over 40 gigabytes of storage capacity on disk drives. Agencies purchasing such systems need to tailor their operational concepts and procedures to manage the use of storage effectively. If, for instance, a PDA has 8 GB of flash memory on a removable disk then issuing multiple flash memory units to an officer would permit an almost unlimited number of collections of biometric samples per shift. On the other hand if a device has a fixed memory storage capacity then the department should determine how much space is available for fingerprints, facial images, and iris images and advise the persons using the Mobile ID devices on how to factor these limitations into the use of the device.

A.2.3 Displays

Displays on standalone capture devices vary from graphical overlays to small displays capable of showing return messages and photographs. Capture devices intended for outdoor, rugged environments must be capable of displaying images and text in bright sunlight as well as in the dark. Sunlight visible means capability for either a front-lit technology or 1000 NITS minimum backlighting. For viewing in the dark, a minimum of 100 NITS of back or front lighting is required. Application software typically enables multiple preset brightness settings and color schemes for daytime versus nighttime viewing.

Note that depending on the Use Case and the modality, it may not be possible or appropriate to return the results of a search to the same device on which they were captured. In such cases an associated PDA style device or laptop in a nearby vehicle may typically be used to display the returned information or matching image(s).

A.2.4 Audio Feedback

Stand alone capture devices have the capability to generate audio or haptic feedback to the operator. Some devices provide equivalent feedback using a vibration in the device.

A.2.5 Expansion Capability

PDA or PC based mobile identification typically support expansion capabilities through one or more of the following interfaces:
- USB host ports, either USB 1.1 or USB 2.0
- USB client port, typically USB 1.1
- Serial port
- PCMCIA slot (type II x 1)
- Mini PCI Express
- SD slot
- Wireless connectivity (discussed below)

A.3   Capture Device Features

A.3.1 General

The following capture device features are considered desirable but not mandatory.

A.3.2 Fingerprint Capture

A.3.2.1 Finger Guide

Fingerprint capture devices with integrated finger guide are desirable to optimize placement of the finger such that the core and first crease of large thumbs is captured. This may also assist in reducing sequence errors. Finger guides can also protect the fingerprint capture area from direct sunlight if required.

A.3.2.2 Finger Location Indicator

Mobile devices with the capability to detect the location of the fingerprint are desirable to provide a left/right, up/down indication for the operator or subject to insure optimal image content.

A.3.2.3 Auto-capture of image

Mobile devices with the capability to evaluate each image frame captured are desirable to determine if a fingerprint is present that meets quality requirements and automatically save the image.

A.3.2.4 Manual capture of image

Mobile devices with the capability to manually command the device to capture the image currently on the sensor are desirable to insure the ability to capture difficult to image fingers.

A.3.2.5 Quality check function

After capture of the fingerprint images, a quality check function is desirable based on a combination of:
1.	Image size
2.	Light or dark image measurements
3.	Minutiae count
4.	Core location
5.	NIST Image quality scores

A.3.2.6 Finger print image display

Display of fingerprints on mobile device during the capture process is a useful option for some mobile device applications.

A.3.2.7 Image Enhancement Features

Image enhancing membranes on optical scanners are desirable to improve the ability to capture dry fingers. Membrane materials include silicon pads, epoxy, and urethane coatings.

A.3.2.8 Platen/Coating replacement

Optical scanner platen surfaces that may be field replaced are desirable to ensure continuity of use.

A.3.2.9 Other Considerations

Aside from the recommendations and requirements listed above for the fingerprint capture device, other factors that affect the performance of these Mobile ID devices and systems need to be considered. Many of these relate to training and include:

- Operation of the device within the temperature and humidity specifications
- Ruggedness of the device
- Officer safety while using
- Use of clean fingers when possible
- Maintain clean platens
- Types of cleaners allowed on platen
- Consistent placement of the same finger(s)
- Consistent centering and use the same area from the flat of the finger
- Optical scanners should avoid excess illumination (or use capture devices that can function effectively in full sunlight)
- If enrolling more than 1 finger, ensure that sequence errors do not occur.
- If enrolling more than 1 finger always reflect accurately which finger is being captured
- On single finger capture devices, sequence errors need to be avoided (especially for enrollments)
- Quality feedback to operator
- How quickly can prints be captured
- How many transactions can be in process simultaneously (can a new set of fingerprints be captured while waiting for search results?)

A.3.3 Facial Capture

A.3.3.1 On Board Illumination (Flash)

Mobile identification devices using PDAs typically provide LED illumination. This illumination is sufficient for images to associate with the return information.

Mobile ID devices used for facial recognition provide a high quality flash function as found on commercial or professional cameras.

A.3.3.2 Docking Station

Download of high resolution images from commercial or professional grade cameras requires a high speed transfer. Docking stations for the camera provide a high speed interface to a PC for transfer to a central location.

A.3.3.3 Return Data Display

Mobile ID devices using facial recognition typically return a photo line up of potential matches to the operator. In many scenarios where face recognition is used in this way the display on the capture device is not adequate for an objective decision to be made and so the potential matches are returned to a laptop or PC (perhaps located in a nearby patrol car) for display on a higher resolution screen.

In cases where a single image is returned (perhaps in verification scenarios where the device is used in conjunction with an ID card or token containing a facial biometric) the display on a PDA style device may be perfectly acceptable.

A.3.4 Iris Capture

A.3.4.1 Transmission of templates/images

Iris templates and images are small enough that transmission can be accomplished using sync cables or wireless connections.

A.3.4.2 Display of results

Display of captured images is helpful in that it provides direct feedback to the operator in the case that iris image quality is not adequate. Results displayed may range from textual demographics data to photographic images.

A.3.4.3 Illumination consideration

Use of sunshields or hoods can facilitate outdoor capture and reduce the need for high-power illumination sources.

A.4 Textual data entry

A.4.1 Keyboards/Keypads

Demographic entry may be accomplished using on screen keyboards, PDA keyboards or keypads, or PC keyboards.

A.4.2 Magnetic Stripe Readers

A magnetic stripe reader with capability of reading driver's licenses per AAMVA DL/ID-2005, enable demographic data entry using these cards.

A.4.3 Bar Code Readers

1-D and 2-D bar codes are used on some identification cards such as driver's licenses. Bar code readers allow input of demographic data from these cards.

In some instances, a 2-D bar code reader may also store fingerprint templates as input for verification.

A.4.4 Smart Card Reader

Smart card reader (contact or contactless) may be used for demographic data entry, for downloading, or storage of templates (fingerprint, facial, or iris) for matching on-board verification devices.

A.4.5 MRZ Reader

In applications using smart cards the information on the passport may include biometrics in compliance with ICAO standards. An MRZ reader, if present in a Mobile ID device, should be able to read an ICAO compliant Machine Readable Zone, in the three different document formats (ID1, ID2 and ID3) defined in ISO/IEC 7810:2003. Optical Character Reader (OCR) software should be integrated in the device, able to analyze the MRZ image and return its content in terms of ASCII characters.

A.5 Power Features

A.5.1 Removable Battery

The ability to remove the battery (or "hot swap") without the loss of stored data or programs allows continuous operation without the need for charging cradles in vehicles.

A.5.2 Charging

The ability to charge from a variety of sources including automotive +12 VDC (+10.0 to +18.0), or from a military vehicle operating off of 24system, or from chargers running on recognized international power sources (110 to 240 VAC) gives flexibility to operator workflows. Units are typically able to operate while charging. Power filtering and surge protection are recommended.

A.5.2.1 Battery Life Indicators

Battery life indicators that display the amount of battery power and estimated time of operation remaining are desirable.

A.5.2.2 Battery Charge Indication

Battery charge indicators that show charging is in process are desirable.

A.5.2.3 Desktop Battery Charger

Desktop battery chargers are typically available. Desktop chargers, car chargers, and devices using a common connector to the Mobile ID device are desirable.

A.5.2.4 Vehicle Charger

Vehicle chargers that operate from car cigarette lighters are desirable.

A.5.2.5 Gang Charger

Gang chargers for charging multiple batteries are desirable.

A.5.3 RAM Holdover Battery

Holdover batteries providing power to on board RAM for up to 30 days are desirable.

A.5.4 Non-Volatile Memory

Application programs stored in non-volatile memory are desirable to prevent loss of applications during a total loss of battery.

A.6 Certifications

Mobile device certifications available include:

US FCC class B part 15
CE Certification
EN 60529, Ingress Protection
    Multiple levels of ingress protection are available.
    Military devices are typically IP65, dust tight and able to survive water spray.
Some naval devices add IP67, dust tight, water tight to 1 meter

Annex B Acquisition Planning
(Informative)

This is not intended to provide all of the considerations for starting a mobile identification project as all implementations are different. They are:

Network: Field devices not accessing a resident database or one in the car needs to be reliable and utilize a bandwidth that can support a response within time frames that are deemed within legal detention time frames.

Network / Manual data transfer: Devices accessing a resident database or one in the car need to be kept current this is either network or done manually (portable media or direct on the device).

Responses: Whenever possible, the operator response should optionally include photos with hit notifications. Photos and candidate lists can be useful when the system cannot provide a positive identification. These could add another level of verification for the operator of the device. Additionally, including warrant information with the response based on the ABIS ID is also very useful, however, when confirming a hit, operators should follow their agency's Standard Operating Procedures.

Training: Operators should be trained in the use of the device. Their testimony in court should be limited to this expertise.

Reporting: Allow for some kind of print out compatible file that can be saved downloaded and then added to a report, citation, or used for court purposes.

E-Citation: If your agency has e-citations, the sensor utilized should meet the minimum specifications in this document. This can aid in having an image that can be enrolled into an AFIS.

Legal: To stay within the limits of existing case law, agencies should adopt an Appropriate Use Policy suitable for their agency mission.

Software updates: As these devices are deployed, they will inevitably require updates. Updating of devices manually is time intensive. Auto updates are recommended.

References

Advanced Encryption Standard FIPS 197; http://csrc.nist.gov/publications/PubsFIPS.html

American Association of Motor Vehicle Administrators Standard (AAMVA DL/ID 2005); http://www.aamva.org/KnowledgeCenter/Standards/Current/DL-IDStandard2005.htm

ANSI/NIST-ITL 1-2007, Data Format for the Interchange of Fingerprint Facial, & Other Biometric Information – Part 1 ; http://fingerprint.nist.gov/standard/index.htm

ANSI/NIST-ITL 2-2008, Data Format for the Interchange of Fingerprint Facial, & Other Biometric Information – Part 2: XML; http://fingerprint.nist.gov/standard/index.htm

ANSI/NIST-ITL 1-2000, Data Format for the Interchange of Fingerprint, Facial, & Scar Mark and Tattoo (SMT) Information; http://fingerprint.nist.gov/standard/archived_workshops/index.html

Electronic Biometrics Transmission Specification, EBTS, Version 8.1, 2008; http://www.fbibiospecs.org/fbibiometric/ebts.html

Electronic Fingerprint Transmission Specification, EFTS, Version 7.1, 2005; http://www.fbibiospecs.org/fbibiometric/ebts.html

EN 60529 Specification for degrees of protection provided by enclosures; http://webstore.ansi.org/FindStandards.aspx?SearchString=IEC+60529&SearchOption=0&Page

FIPS 140-1: Security Requirements for Cryptographic Modules; http://csrc.nist.gov/publications/PubsFIPS.html

FIPS 180-2 Secure Hash Standard (SHS) * Superceded By: FIPS 180 -3 ; http://csrc.nist.gov/publications/PubsFIPSArch.html

FIPS 186-3 DRAFT Digital Signature Standard (DSS); http://csrc.nist.gov/publications/PubsFIPS.html

IEC 825 Eye safety classification of some consumer electronic products; http://ieeexplore.ieee.org/xpl/freeabs_all.jsp?arnumber=543110

International Civil Aviation Organization (ICAO) ; http://csrc.nist.gov/publications/PubsFIPSArch.html

INCITS 378:2004 - American National Standard for Information Technology — Finger Minutiae Format for Data Interchange

INCITS 381:2004 - American National Standard for Information Technology — Finger Image-Based Data Interchange Format

IP xx Ingress Protection Rating; http://www.mpl.ch/info/IPratings.html

ISO/IEC 10918-1 Digital Compression and Coding of Continuous-Tone Still Images Part 1: Requirements and Guidelines (JPEG)

ISO/IEC 19794-2:2004 Information Technology- Biometric data interchange formats- Part : Finger Minutiae Data

ISO/IEC 19794-4:2004 Information Technology- Biometric data interchange formats- Part : Finger Image Data

ISO/IEC 19794-5:2004 Information Technology- Biometric data interchange formats- Part : Face Image Data

ISO/IEC 19794-6:2004 Information Technology- Biometric data interchange formats- Part : Iris Image Data

MIL-STD-810F; http://www.dtc.army.mil/navigator

Minutiae Interoperability Exchange Test (MINEX); http://fingerprint.nist.gov/minex04/index.html

National Information Exchange Model (NIEM 2.0) ; http://www.niem.gov/library.php

NIEM XML; http://www.niem.gov/xmlSchemas.php

WSQ Gray-scale Fingerprint Image Compression Specification, Dec., 1997; http://www.fbibiospecs.org/fbibiometric/biometric_specs.html

Acronyms/Glossary

ACRONYM	MEANING
ABIS	Automated Biometric Identification System
AFIS	Automated Fingerprint Identification System
ANSI/NIST	American National Standards Institute / National Institute of Standards and Technology
ARM	Advanced RISC Machine
BAP	Biometric Application Profile
BPR	Best Practice Recommendation
CDMA/1XRTT	Code Division Multiple Access technology
CE	Officially known as Windows Embedded Compact Windows CE is Microsoft's operating system for minimalistic computers and embedded systems
CPU	Central Processing Unit
dB	Decibels
DHS	Department of Homeland Security
DoD	Department of Defense
DSP	Digital Signal Processors
DSS	Digital Signature Standard
EBTS	Electronic Biometric Transmission Specification
EDGE	Enhanced Data Rates for Global Evolution
EFTS	Electronic Fingerprint Transmission Specification
EVDO/EVDM	EVDO and EVDM are 3G iterations of the CDMA technology that push data rates up to 1 megabits/sec
FBI	Federal Bureau of Investigation
FIPS	Federal Information Processing Standard
FPS	Frames per second
FTA	Failure to acquire
GPRS	Global Packet Radio Services
GPS	Global Positioning System
GSM	Global System for Mobile
HSDPA/WCDMA	The next phase of cellular technology to approach 40 megabytes/sec
IAFIS	Integrated Automated Fingerprint Identification System
ID	Identification

ACRONYM	MEANING
IP	Internet Protocol
IP XX	Ingress Protection Rating
IREX	Iris Exchange evaluation
ISO	International Standards Organization
IT	Information Technology
ITL	Information Technology Laboratory (NIST)
JPEG	Joint Photographic Expert Group
KST	Known or Suspected Terrorist
LED	Light emitting diode
MINEX	Minutiae Exchange evaluation
MRZ	Machine Readable Zone
ms	millisecond
NCIC	National Crime Information Center
NET	The *.NET* Framework is Microsoft's comprehensive and consistent programming model for building applications
NFIQ	NIST Fingerprint Image Quality
NGI	Next Generation Identification
NIEM	National Information Exchange Model
NIST	National Institute of Standards & Technology
nm	Nanometer
OCR	Optical Character Recognition Optical Character Reader
OS	Operating System
PC	Personal Computer
PCI	Peripheral Component Interface
PDA	Personal Digital Assistant
PIV	Personal Identity Verification
PIX	Private Internet Exchange
ppi	pixels per inch
R&D	Research and Development
RAM	Random Access Memory
RGB	Red Green Blue
RISC	Repository for Individuals of Special Concern
SAP	Subject Acquisition Profile
SD	Type of data storage card
MTs	Scars, Marks, and Tattoos
TWIC	Transportation Worker Identification Credential
USB	Universal Serial Bus
US FCC	United States Federal Communications Commission
US VISIT	United States Visitor and Immigrant Status Indicator

ACRONYM	MEANING
	Technology
VAC	Volts AC
VDC	Volts DC
WCDMA	The next phase of cellular technology to approach 40 megabytes/sec
WSQ	Wavelet Scalar Quantization
XML	Extensible Markup Language